Have I ever told you
how glad I am
that you're my sister?
I'm telling you now
because I want you to know
how very important
    you are to me
and just how much love
    there is for you
        deep within my heart.

— Deanne Laura Gilbert

Blue Mountain Arts®

Bestselling Titles

By Susan Polis Schutz
To My Daughter with Love on the Important Things in Life
To My Son with Love

By Wally Amos
Be Positive!
The Power of Self-Esteem

By Donna Fargo
I Prayed for You Today
Ten Golden Rules for Living in This Crazy, Mixed-Up World

By Douglas Pagels
100 Things to Always Remember… and One Thing to Never Forget
Every daughter should have a book like this to remind her how wonderful she is
For You, Just Because You're Very Special to Me
May You Always Have an Angel by Your Side
Required Reading for All Teenagers

Anthologies
7 Days to a Positive Attitude
Always Believe in Yourself and Your Dreams
For My Wonderful Mother
For You, My Daughter
God Is Always Watching Over You
Hang In There
Keep Believing in Yourself and Your Dreams
The Love Between a Mother and Daughter Is Forever
There Is Greatness Within You, My Son
Think Positive Thoughts Every Day

I'm Glad You Are My Sister

A Blue Mountain Arts® Collection

Edited by Gary Morris

Blue Mountain Press ™

Boulder, Colorado

Library of Congress Catalog Card Number: 00-057396

ISBN: 0-88396-562-3

ACKNOWLEDGMENTS appear on page 64.

Certain trademarks are used under license.
Blue Mountain Press is registered in U.S. Patent and Trademark Office.
Printed in the United States of America.
Sixth Printing: 2008

 This book is printed on recycled paper.

This book is printed on fine quality, laid embossed paper. This paper has been specially produced to be acid free (neutral pH) and contains no groundwood or unbleached pulp. It conforms with all the requirements of the American National Standards Institute, Inc., so as to ensure that this book will last and be enjoyed by future generations.

Library of Congress Cataloging-in-Publication Data

I'm glad you are my sister : a Blue Mountain Arts collection.
     p. cm.
     ISBN 978-0-88396-562-7 (alk. paper)
     1. Sisters—Poetry. 2. Brothers and sisters—Poetry.
  3. American poetry—20th century. I. SPS Studios (Firm)

PS595.S57 I4 2000
811.008'0352045—dc21

                                                              00-057396

Blue Mountain Arts, Inc.
P.O. Box 4549, Boulder, Colorado 80306

Contents

I'm Glad You Are My Sister

Have I ever told you
how glad I am
that you're my sister?
I'm telling you now
because I want you to know
how very important
  you are to me
and just how much love
    there is for you
      deep within my heart.
Too often,
the beautiful things in life
are taken for granted,
and I realize that you
are one of the most beautiful
aspects of mine.

That's why it's so important
   for me to tell you now
that you are special to me.
You're more than just family;
you are a friend,
a confidante,
and a shoulder to lean on
   in times of need.
You're the person I always
   want to share everything with —
each dream,
each goal I attain,
each sorrow,
each joy.
If I have never told you before
how glad I am
that you're my sister,
I'm telling you now.
I want you to know
that you mean the world to me,
and I love you
with all my heart.

— Deanne Laura Gilbert

*W*hen it comes to our feelings
    for each other,
we're not always very expressive.
We share our thoughts,
spend hours talking, exchanging opinions,
and telling each other everything,
but somehow those mutual feelings
    aren't mentioned.
Instead, they're safely stored inside
    our hearts,
because we know that they'll be kept
    perfectly in that loving place.
We don't need words to talk about
our love and friendship for each other.
We can share our feelings with smiles
    and hugs and happy times together.

— Barbara J. Hall

Sister, Here Are Some
Things You Never Knew

You're more than just a sister to me.
You're like summer in my heart.
Warming everything.
Encouraging my world to blossom and grow.

You let me know that smiles are to be expected,
and gifts like honesty, closeness, laughter, and
kind, open-minded communication will always
breeze into my life through the open doors that
you lovingly hold the key to.

My life would be so much less if you weren't
in it. I'm sorry if I haven't expressed that
thought as much as I should have. There are
probably too many special things that I've let
go unsaid.

But of all the things you never
knew, I want to say now that every
passing year fills my world —
and my heart —

with more and more love
...for you.

— Marin McKay

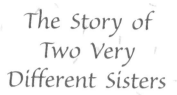

The Story of Two Very Different Sisters

One is here, one lives there. One is a little taller than the other. Two different colors of hair, two different outlooks on life, two very different views from their windows. Both have different tomorrows ahead. Each is unique in so many ways. Each has her own story, with all the busy things going on in the present. Each has different work to do and different demands on the day. Each has a separate destination and a distinctly different path to get there. But...

For all the things that might be
different and unique about them…
these two sisters will always share so
much. They will always be the best of
family _and_ friends, entwined together,
through all the days of their lives.
Their love will always be very special:
gentle and joyful when it can be,
strong and giving when it needs to
be, reminding them, no matter how
different their stories turn out…
they share the incredibly precious gift
of being "sisters." And when you
think of some of the best things this
world has to offer, a blessing like
that is really… what it's all about.

— Laurel Atherton

We Have Been Given
a Wonderful Gift...

We have been given the chance
to experience the wonders of life
together.

The good times I treasure the most,
and some of the best memories I have,
were spent with you.
In the worst times,
we only became stronger.

I want you to know that
in difficult times
I will not stand behind you
or walk in front of you;
I will walk beside you,
and I will always be there.

No distance
or person
can take away
what we have or who we are,
because you are my sister...
        always.

— Gwendolyn Moore

A Sister's Heart Is a Memory Box Full of Moments to Treasure

You bring so much tenderness and caring
to the hearts of those around you,
and I want you to know that I cherish
our special times together.
When I want a little sisterly advice,
your understanding is just the answer I need.
When I'm after a positive outlook,
your caring brightens my day.
Your ability to believe in others
and help them stand tall and straight
makes you such a wonderful person.
Your warm touches from the heart
make you such a remarkable woman.
Your kind, generous nature
and laughter through the years
make you such a precious sister.
Your love for life and everyone
makes you such a special friend.
More than anything else,
I'll always remember your love.

— Linda E. Knight

My Sister Is...

My sister is my heart.
She opens doors to rooms
I never knew were there,
Breaks through walls
I don't recall building.
She lights my darkest corners
With the sparkle in her eyes.

My sister is my soul.
She inspires my wearied spirit
To fly on wings of angels,
But while I hold her hand
My feet never leave the ground.
She stills my deepest fears
With the wisdom of her song.

My sister is my past.
She writes my history.
In her eyes I recognize myself;
I have memories only we can share.
She remembers, she forgives,
And she accepts me as I am —
With tender understanding.

My sister is my future.
She lives within my dreams.
She sees my undiscovered secrets,
Believes in me as I stumble.
She walks in step with me,
Her love lighting my way.

My sister is my strength.
She hears the whispered prayers
That I cannot speak.
She helps me find my smile,
Freely giving hers away.
She catches my tears
In her gentle hands.

My sister is like no one else.
She's my most treasured friend —
Filling up the empty spaces,
Healing broken places.
She is my rock, my inspiration.
Though impossible to define,
In a word, she is… my sister.

— Lisa Lorden

If I gathered up all my wishes for you
and put them in a pretty basket, your
multicolored bouquet would look like this...

You'd have peace from every conflict you
encounter in your life, all the love you
need, and perfect health to enjoy this
journey of life. Your basket would be filled
with dreams come true, goals met, and
satisfaction with your achievements.

There would be many friendships to
enhance your feeling of community and
belonging. A variety of meaningful
relationships gives life spice and balance, so
I'd fill your basket with the kind of friends
you can call on, go places with, and care for.

There would be prayers for your freedom from everything that binds you and solutions to any problems you may have in life. In this pretty basket of wishes, you would have everything you need and want, and every situation and circumstance you encounter would enhance your potential for happiness.

May the time and concern you've invested in others translate into the kind of love and appreciation for yourself that you so deserve. You are worthy. You are beautiful. You are loved.

As I stir through the memories of what we've shared through the years, I want you to know that... I wish you love, I wish you happiness, and I hope your every dream is coming true.

— Donna Fargo

If Ever You Need Me,
I'll Be There...

If ever you need a helping hand,
   just reach out and touch mine.

If ever you're scared or afraid,
   I'll be right by your side.

If ever you need words of advice,
   I'll give you the best I have.

If ever you're sad and depressed,
   I'll try to brighten your day.

If ever you need a shoulder to cry on,
   I have two, waiting here for you.

If ever you simply need to talk,
   I promise I'll sit and listen.

Whatever the reason,
whatever you're searching for,
whatever you need...

I promise
        I'll always be there
                for you.

— Erin N. Himelrick

You're Always Welcome...
in My Heart

You don't have to be perfect to belong in this place. You don't have to have all the answers, or always know the right thing to say. You can climb the highest mountain, if you want. Or quietly imagine that you might, someday. You can take chances or take safety nets, make miracles or make mistakes. You don't have to be composed at all hours to be strong here. You don't have to be bold or certain to be brave. You don't have to have all the answers here, or even know who you want to be...

just take my hand
and rest your heart
and stay awhile with me.

— Ashley Rice

A Sister Is Nature's Way
of Making Sure
We Always Have a Friend

From the time we were old enough
    to know what friendship meant,
we knew we were destined to be
    the best of friends.
We played together, laughed together,
    and dreamed together.
Having someone to share the most
    important times in my life
has meant more to me than
    you could ever know.
It seems as if you always know
    just when I need you,
and you're there — always
    and without hesitation.

You never judge me or criticize me,
even though there are times
    in my life when
I certainly need some criticism.
You are the one who is always
    supporting me
in making whatever decisions
    I choose to make,
encouraging me as I follow through,
cheering me on when I succeed,
and picking me up when I fail.
No other friend has ever been
    so faithful.
Knowing that you'll always be here
    on my side,
loving, supporting, and being
    my best friend,
makes every star seem so much
    more reachable.
I love you, Sister.

— Kimberly D. Boren

I Love the Times
I Spend with You

No matter the time or place,
moments spent with you
are always special.

Even as they are happening,
our times together are
filling my heart with
precious memories.

We have quiet moments
and louder ones, too.
Then there are the laughable
times when I forget myself

There are moments when I learn
something new about you,
or even myself,
and moments when we're just
content to be together.

Our moments together are
varied and full, and
I cherish each one for a
different reason.

I love being with you,
and when our moments together
are through,
I hold you close in my heart,
for always.

— Linda Sackett-Morrison

Family Is the Best
Feeling in the World

The best feeling in this world
   is family.
From it, we draw love,
   friendship, moral support,
and the fulfillment of every
   special need within our hearts.
In a family, we are connected to
   an ever-present source
of sunny moments, smiles and laughter,
understanding and encouragement,
and hugs that help us grow in confidence
   all along life's path.
Wherever we are, whatever we're doing,
whenever we really need to feel
   especially loved, befriended,
      supported, and cared for
         in the greatest way,
our hearts can turn to the family
and find the very best
   always waiting for us.

— Barbara J. Hall

We Are Family!

We can be ourselves with each other.
We share family and memories
and know each other completely.
We share secrets and dreams
and accept each other
just as we are.
We can laugh and giggle about anything;
we share a sense of humor
    that is unique to us.
We count on each other
    and help one another.
In the darkest hour,
    we can see the light
as long as we're looking for it
    together.
We understand one another
    as no one else can.
We listen and care.
We accept, even when we don't agree.
We're a special combination
    of friends and family,
and the bond of love we share
    is forever.

— Barbara Cage

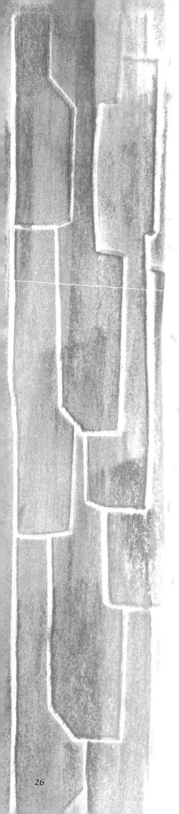

Some Reminders
from the Family
That Loves You

Remember always…

…that for all your strength,
there is much that remains
far beyond your control.

…that you are but a spoke in a
magnificent wheel
that eternally rotates,
but you are never forgotten
and never replaced.

…that for each loss in your world,
there is yet something to be gained…
or someone.

Remember always…

…that you have much to forgive,
much to achieve,
much to heal,
and much to mend.

…that these are the things
that will make you
strong, happy, fulfilled,
and complete.

…that you are loved,
wholly and forever,
and it is that force
which you may draw upon
at any time
and for any duration.

…that all of this is truth
because we are your family,
and we will be here for you.

— T. Marien

May You Have a Home
Filled with Love

Home is the place where you can be
Totally yourself
Without any need
For pretense or defense
Without any need for protection

Home is where you can be vulnerable
Without any fear of disapproval
You can relax — feel the comfort of silence
Without fear of rejection or criticism

Home is where you can trust your instincts most
To provide truth, justice, and insight
You can listen to your intuition
Without explanation
Without a need for atonement or motive

Home is where you can give without taking
Love without making apologies for
Your mistakes
You can be simple or complicated
Without rationalization or justification

Home is where you find inspiration
Where silence encourages your creativity
And a word can awaken your dreams
Where a feeling means everything

Home is where you can allow yourself to change
To grow and become the person you hope to be
You can be free of society's standards
Listen to your inner guide
Without any anxiety

Home is where your soul is free
Where you can be yourself
Home is where your heart is
Because
Home is where love lives
Unconditionally

— Regina Hill

*S*istering isn't easy…
One always has to be the older one,
"big sister" — born first, first to try
two-wheelers, make-up, dates; first to
stay up late; first to face the challenges
of life, the one to go to for comfort
and advice.

The other always has to be the
younger one, "little sister" — never
quite catching up in the race, seeing
her future self in another's face;
always in the shadow of her sister,
always measured by her shining list
of grades and past successes, always
wearing "hand-me-down" dresses.

We didn't always want to share a room,
or clothes, or friends, or even our last
name!
Each wanted to outshine the other…
winning pride from Dad and praise
from Mother.

The only thing we never got a chance to share while
growing up...
    was being the same age at the same stage
    of life... something real friends share.

Years later...
    both of us have families of our own, and
    suddenly we're so much more than simply
    sisters, as we were before:
we're wives and mothers,
    sharing joys and fears, and even tears;
    we're women,
journeying through life, able to commiserate,
    learning to appreciate our special bond.
All that we shared uneasily as children
    has brought us closer now that we're both grown,
    each knowing what the other's also known.

And so, dear Sister,
    while it's thought a compliment to tell a friend,
    "You're like a sister to me"...
between us,
    it's my heart's simple truth: "You are a real friend
    to me, and all that I've become you've helped me
    learn to be."

— Beth Thompson

Let's Be
Little Sisters Again

Let's build sand castles
   where kings and queens live;
      we'll make little windows
         with our fingertips.
Let's play dress-up;
   you can be the princess,
      and I'll wear purple flowers
         and bring some tea.
Let's dance in the puddles,
   wear yellow galoshes,
      taste the rain as it falls
         from the sky.
Let's make frosty angels,
   bury ourselves in the snow,
      and, with our make-believe wings,
         fly far, far away.
Let's forget our responsibilities.
   Let's forget that we have grown up.
      Let's be little sisters again.

— Diane Mastromarino

As Sisters,
we have a special bond that
can't be broken by time,
distance, or the Inconveniences of
life. We share secrets, hopes,
dreams, and fantasies that no one
else knows — Sometimes with
laughter, sometimes through tears,
always with love — just because
we're sisters. That means we
can disagree about the smallest things
or be serious rivals, but it
doesn't last. Even talking
badly about each other is allowed,
but only sisters get that
privilege on very Rare occasions —
certain that nothing and no one
can ever really come between
us. You See, nothing is
more important than being sisters, and…

no sister is more important
than you!

— Andrea L. Hines

No One Is
Closer to Me
than You

We don't look alike,
we don't share the same interests,
and quite often we don't think
    the same way...
No wonder people are surprised
when they learn we are family.
We are two opposites...
    like denim and lace,
two separate peas
    from a common pod,
yet no one is closer to my heart.
Sometimes in amusement,
and sometimes in amazement,
I look at you and wonder how
we could be so different,
but most of the time I think
we complement each other.

I admire in you the qualities
I desire for myself but do not have.
You encourage me to follow my heart,
even though it travels a path
opposite from your own.
You support me in the decisions I make,
even though they are different
from those you would make.
When I make a foolish mistake,
you resist the temptation to say
"I told you so."
Given our differences,
our relationship
could have been cool or distant,
but we chose to be friends and
to love each other without reservation.
You have added spice and color
and endless variety to my life,
and I love you more
than words can say.

— Patricia A. Teckelt

A sister is...
  sharing cookies and a glass of milk,
  riding the school bus home together,
  playing dolls and dress-up,
arguing over whose turn it is
  to set the dinner table,
and swapping your favorite books.

A sister is...
  sharing a cup of coffee,
   and splitting the muffin (fewer calories!),
  driving in the car to Mom's house,
 going shopping together for clothes,
  watching each other's kids,
arguing over whose turn it is
  to have Thanksgiving dinner at her house,
and swapping your favorite books.

  We've both grown up
  and live our own lives now,
  but as each year passes by,
 I realize
that most important of all...

A sister is...
  forever.

      — Paula Holmes-Eber

I Am Happy
to Have You as
Part of My World

You have a wonderful way
of looking at the world
of making everything beautiful
of seeing the little things
for more than they are
Creativity flows from you as you
paint the world with imagination
Your palette is your mind
and your presence, a brush
flooding everything around you
with exuberant color
Just being around you inspires me
to look at life differently
to appreciate the good in things, and
to feel what it means to really live
You love your place in the world
and you make others love theirs, too
You catch fireflies and follow rainbows
smell flowers and find shapes in the clouds
You live your life to the fullest
and I am happy to have you
as part of my world

— Diane Mastromarino

Follow Your Dreams, Because They Are Beautiful

When I look at you and how you've grown and changed over the years, I am always caught by the sense of how proud I am — of who you are, and of the special place you have in my heart and in my life. You are a woman of dreams, whose heart and vision are so big that you touch the lives of those around you without even trying.

You are generous, compassionate, and understanding. You are real; I guess that's one of the things I love most about you. You know how to share your feelings, and you care about the feelings of others. I feel safe with you.

That is why it is so important for me
to encourage you right now, when I know
that you are venturing out on some new
ground... and trying out your wings.
I feel that you are a little hesitant right
now, not sure if your dreams are strong
enough to take you where you want to
go. I need you to see that they are.
They are attainable, because they are
beautiful. They are yours. They come from
your heart, which is good and honest and
strong and kind, and so they need to
come true. They will benefit others.
You are my sister; you are also my friend.
I believe in you and your dreams. Follow
them, because — like you, Sister — they
are beautiful.

— donna reames

May you always find warmth
in the hands reaching out
to wish you happiness.
May your hard work
make all the moments of effort
   and sacrifice
seem more than worthwhile.
Always know how proud I am
that you dare to live out
   your dreams.

I hope that your life will be
   full and rich and blessed.
I admire the person that you are
and the woman you've become —
one who is not afraid to
   clearly define
her values and beliefs.
My deepest desire is that
   your strong self-image
will continue to grow
and that you will celebrate
   great achievements.

— Linda E. Knight

I Hope Every Day
of Your Life Brings You...

Freedom and honesty...
   to truly get to know yourself and what you want
   in life.

Joy and wonder...
   the kind you get from loving someone more
   deeply than you ever dreamed possible and the
   happiness of sharing life with them.

Strength and confidence...
   the kind that comes from those experiences that
   teach you that you can rely on yourself and you
   do have something to say about your destiny.

Courage and energy...
   to pursue the adventure of exploring your own
   dreams — big or small.

Tolerance, insight, and perspective...
   to see others as they are and let them be,
   along with the gentle openness to learn from them
   and apply what you can to your own life, while
   still maintaining the values that are right for you.

Peace and happiness...
   the kind that comes from knowing you are loved.

— Deeva D. Boleman

I Loved Sharing a Childhood with You

Sometimes a memory from our childhood tickles my thoughts and makes me smile.

Sis, do you remember…

…how we poked and teased each other in the back seat of the car until Dad threatened to turn around and go home?

…Christmas Eves when we couldn't sleep, and we lay whispering in the dark, certain we'd heard something on the roof?

...when we chased each other in circles
    around Mom's legs, and she promised to
separate us if we kept it up?

...our first day back to school: the rush, the
    butterflies in our stomachs, the luscious
    smell of new leather shoes?

...those summer nights spent gazing at the
    stars and wondering where they ended?

These are just a few of the memories that
    mean so much because we share them
    together. And now, even though we can't
    see each other every day, you are still in
    my thoughts... and in my heart.

— Emily King

I Look at You, Sister, and I See...

A part of who I am
and who I wish to be.

I face a woman
   who has grown and explored
   and imagined with me.
I see a woman
   who has traveled her own inner journeys
   and continues on her own unique path
      each day.
In you, I face a woman
   I have vigorously fought, challenged,
   and hurt at times.

I see a woman
  who has never deserted, discouraged,
  or forgotten me.
I face a woman
  who acknowledges my anger and fears
  and leads me toward a peace within.
I see a woman
  who teaches me and shares with me
  and encourages me to grow.
I face a woman
  who is her own vibrant self
  and a deep spiritual believer.
I see you, my sister…
    my truest friend,
    my deepest strength,
    and my greatest blessing.

— Kathleen F. Foley

To One of the Most
Beautiful People I Know

You have a beautiful heart that overflows with love and life. You are such a great inspiration, and I just had to tell you.

You seem to have a joy in your heart at all times. Your happiness rubs off on others, and it affects me. I can't help but feel happy when I'm around you.

Your enthusiasm is contagious. You are excited about everything. A person cannot be interested in all the facets of life without having a loving and beautiful heart... and you do.

In order to care, there must be a depth of love and concern for all of humanity. You have it. It's in your beautiful heart and in your very soul. This makes you rare, indeed.

Today, I just wanted to let you know what a great contribution you make to the lives of all those who know you... especially me.

— Barbara Dager Kohen

Today and Every Day...
Celebrate Your Life!

Soar with the eagles today. Let your spirit take you high. Face any hills or mountains with a victorious attitude... without worry, without dread. Let go of any troubles you have. See yourself released, free, running in the meadow of life, like a little child. Visualize doors opening for you that you haven't been able to open. See yourself being embraced by everyone with whom you come in contact. You're special. Believe it. Take time for yourself today.

Eat your favorite food today. Call your favorite person. Do whatever would make you happiest. Pull open the drapes from around the windows of your heart. Reach out. Be willing to receive. Take it easy. If something starts to ruffle your feathers, adjust your attitude, just like you would adjust the heat or air in your house or car. Be comfortable. Tell the universe and yourself that you're taking this day off for yourself, that your other duties and chores will just have to wait. Realize that you're so important and special to those who know you and love you. Today is your day to celebrate!

— Donna Fargo

You Are
So Important to Me

You're important to me because we share
many of the same ideas and beliefs —
and even when we don't, we respect the
other's opinion.

You're important to me because we share
memories of childhood struggles, teenage
rebellion, and adult responsibilities. Those
memories are unique to you and me.

You're important to me because we share
laughter. Sometimes we share regular
laughter, but at times we laugh over
things that no one but us can find the
humor in. That's my favorite kind of
laughter, and you are my favorite person
to share it with.

You're important to me because we share tears.
Sometimes they are regular tears, but at
times they are private ones that only we
can share and understand. Those are the
most important kind, and I'm thankful that
I have you to share them with.

You're important to me because we can share any
    secret and know that whether or not we agree
    with it, it is in safe-keeping. I know that I can
    tell you things I could never tell anyone else.
You're important to me because we share
    our hopes and dreams. When we share them,
    we each know that we have someone who
    supports us, believes in what we want, and
    who will hope as much as we do that our
    dreams come true.
You are so important to me; there isn't a person
    in the world who could ever take your place
    in my life.
There is no one I'd rather laugh or cry with
    or share my innermost thoughts with, and
    there is absolutely no one I'd rather have as
    my sister.

— Barbara Cage

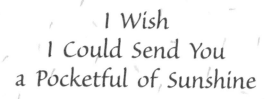

I Wish
I Could Send You
a Pocketful of Sunshine

If I could reach up
    and touch the sky,
I would catch a rainbow
    full of color
and put it in my pocket.
Then when your world was gray,
I would take it out
and put it in your hand.

If I could walk the meadows
    from here to there,
I would pluck flowers
    of delicate fragrance
and put them in my pocket.
Then when your world
    was falling apart,
I would take them out
    and put them in your hand.

If I could sail the ocean's waves,
I would gather the diamonds
dancing on the spray
and put them in my pocket.
Then when your world needed laughter,
I would take them out
and put them in your hand.

I would do anything
to make your world
a place of sunshine
and happiness.
Just let me know whenever
you need a hug...
because my pockets
are never empty of those.

— Dolores Wyckoff

You Work So Hard
and Do So Much

You work so hard and do so much. And I know that you wonder sometimes — if anyone really appreciates the efforts you make on all those uphill climbs. Day in and day out you make the world a better place to be. And the people who are lucky enough to be in your life are the ones who get to see that you're a very wonderful person with a truly gifted touch. You go a million miles out of your way and you always do so much… to make sure that other lives are easier and filled with happiness. Your caring could never be taken for granted because the people you're close to are blessed… with someone who works at a job well done to bring smiles to the day.

You're a special person who deserves more thanks than this could ever say.

— Jenn Davids

Here Are the Things
I Want for You

I want you to always be happy and to be safe and secure. I want you to be well and at peace with yourself. I want you to get from life all that you desire, and more. I want you to feel free to do whatever you want and to let that freedom soar. I want you to know love and be surrounded by it, to bear no pain and feel no hurt. I want you to be the best person you can be. I want you to share the wonderful gift of yourself with others — how very lucky are those who will receive that beauty!

Above all, I want you to know how very much I care... for you.

— debbie peddle

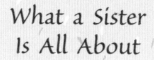

What a Sister
Is All About

My feelings for you wander
back through sunny days when it
felt like we had the whole world
to ourselves. We shared so much,
and we cared more than our
hearts could begin to realize. At
the time, there was so much joy I
took for granted and so many
things I didn't even stop to think
of. But I began to learn how
important you were to my
happiness and that a sister is all
about… love.

As we grew, and time passed by,
we had to begin to choose the
paths our lives would take. It
wasn't easy to know which way to
go and what things to do, but I
was reassured because of the
treasure I held in my heart…

By being my sister, you gave me the quiet comfort of knowing I could always turn to you. That's what a sister is all about... sweetness and support to see you through.

All through our years, you have been a source of so many smiles and so much inspiration for me. There has never been a time when the miles that came between us have not been bridged by the closeness of our hearts. I want to thank you for giving me the special kind of feelings that only you and I could comprehend. That's what we are all about... being the very best of friends.

— Marin McKay

Sister, You Are
a Wonderful Part
of My Life

It's funny — when we were kids,
we never thought we'd even
    like each other,
much less love one another.
But now that we've grown older
    and closer,
I can't imagine my life
    without your being
an important part of it.

Our little chats provide support
    and comfort;
your thoughtful gestures lift
    my spirits;
your dogged determination
    inspires me;
and your kindness touches me
    in ways you couldn't imagine.

When we were young,
   we couldn't understand
      each other's value —
but now we know that having each other
   is the best gift of all.

Today and every day,
   I stop to thank God
      that I have you.
Now I want to thank you...
for being such a wonderful person,
   for putting up with me,
and for being the best sister
   I could ever hope for!

— Donna Gephart

You Are an Extraordinary Woman

Even before I ask,
you're always there for me —
to comfort and to heal me,
to touch and to bless me.
You are so special.
You've brought hope into every situation
and growth into every new challenge.
You've been a shoulder to lean on,
a heart to rely on,
and a voice to cheer me on.
Thank you for sharing yourself,
for the offerings of time
    and conversation.
Thank you for your thoughtfulness,
    caring,
and the touch of your hand
    holding mine tighter.
Thank you for all that you are,
    all that you do,
and all that you have been to me.

— Linda E. Knight

I Am Honored
to Call You My Sister

I know that I can trust you
with my most cherished treasures,
with my heart and soul, and
with every secret I hold.
I know that you will listen
without criticizing me for my mistakes.
You hear what I am trying to say,
even when I fail to express myself clearly.
I know that I can believe you
without worrying that you will mislead me
because you are honest with me,
even when honesty means disagreement.
I know that you will accept me,
despite every wrong turn I've taken
or every bad decision I've made.
You simply love who I am.
I know that our hearts are connected
on the deepest level.
You know me so well;
your insight and your view of me
make me feel complete.
I know that I am special
because you are so special.
I'm proud of our friendship and
the strength we have together.
I am honored to call you my sister
and fortunate to call you my friend.

What Is a Sister?

A sister is someone more special than words. She's love mixed with friendship, the best things in life. She's so much inner beauty blended together with an outward appearance that brings a smile to the happiness in your heart.

A sister is one of the most precious people in the story of your life. And you'll always be together, whether you're near or apart.

Together, you have shared some of the most special moments two people have ever shared. A sister is a perspective on the past, and she's a million favorite memories that will always last.

A sister is a photograph that is one of your most treasured possessions. She's a note that arrives on a special day, and when there's news to share, she's the first one you want to call. A sister is a reminder of the blessings that come from closeness. Sharing secrets. Disclosing dreams. Learning about life together.

A sister is a confidante and a counselor. She's a dear and wonderful friend, and — in certain ways — something like a twin. She's a hand within your hand; she's so often the only one who really understands. A sister is honesty and trust enfolded with love. She's sometimes the only person who sees the horizon from your point of view, and she helps you to see things more clearly. She is a helper and a guide, and she is a feeling, deep inside, that makes you wonder what you would ever do without her.

What is a sister? She's someone more special than words; someone beautiful and unique. And in so many ways, there is no one who is loved so dearly.

— Douglas Pagels

There are three
   simple wishes
that I hold in my heart
   for you.
I wish for you
happiness and special times
for you to enjoy.
I wish for you good health
in everything you do.
But most of all,
I wish for you
the truest love there is
in the world:
the love of family.
I know how much
   that means to you,
because it will always mean
   so much to me.

— Laura Medley

To a Sister Who
Means So Much

When I think about our times growing
up together, I get a warm feeling in
my heart.
I'm grateful for all of it: the secrets, the
arguments, the competitions, and the
accomplishments.
My memories of experiences we've shared
comfort me. When life seems complicated,
I drift back to a time when we enjoyed
simple pleasures that I'm sure we didn't
appreciate at the time.
Now I see all our childhood adventures as
irreplaceable links in a chain that will
hold you close to my heart forever.
No matter how many years pass, no matter
how many miles separate us, those times
we shared and those yet to come make
our relationship a priceless gift.

I'm thankful for you always.

— Michelle M. Boisvert

ACKNOWLEDGMENTS

The following is a partial list of authors whom the publisher especially wishes to thank for permission to reprint their works.

Barbara J. Hall for "When it comes to our feelings…" and "Family Is the Best Feeling in the World." Copyright © 2000 by Barbara J. Hall. All rights reserved. Reprinted by permission.

Lisa Lorden for "My Sister Is…." Copyright © 2000 by Lisa Lorden. All rights reserved. Reprinted by permission.

PrimaDonna Entertainment Corp. for "To My Sister, with Love" by Donna Fargo. Copyright © 1999 by PrimaDonna Entertainment Corp. And for "Today and Every Day… Celebrate Your Life!" by Donna Fargo. Copyright © 2000 by PrimaDonna Entertainment Corp. All rights reserved. Reprinted by permission.

Kimberly D. Boren for "A Sister Is Nature's Way of Making Sure We Always Have a Friend." Copyright © 2000 by Kimberly D. Boren. All rights reserved. Reprinted by permission.

T. Marien for "Some Reminders from the Family That Loves You." Copyright © 2000 by T. Marien. All rights reserved. Reprinted by permission.

Regina Hill for "May You Have a Home Filled with Love" and "I Am Honored to Call You My Sister." Copyright © 2000 by Regina Hill. All rights reserved. Reprinted by permission.

Beth Thompson for "Sistering isn't easy…." Copyright © 2000 by Beth Thompson. All rights reserved. Reprinted by permission.

Diane Mastromarino for "Let's Be Little Sisters Again" and "I Am Happy to Have You as Part of My World." Copyright © 2000 by Diane Mastromarino. All rights reserved. Reprinted by permission.

Andrea L. Hines for "As Sisters…." Copyright © 2000 by Andrea L. Hines. All rights reserved. Reprinted by permission.

Patricia A. Teckelt for "No One Is Closer to Me than You." Copyright © 2000 by Patricia A. Teckelt. All rights reserved. Reprinted by permission.

Paula Holmes-Eber for "A sister is…." Copyright © 2000 by Paula Holmes-Eber. All rights reserved. Reprinted by permission.

donna reames for "Follow Your Dreams, Because They Are Beautiful." Copyright © 2000 by donna reames. All rights reserved. Reprinted by permission.

Emily King for "I Loved Sharing a Childhood with You." Copyright © 2000 by Emily King. All rights reserved. Reprinted by permission.

Kathleen F. Foley for "I Look at You, Sister, and I See…." Copyright © 2000 by Kathleen F. Foley. All rights reserved. Reprinted by permission.

Dolores Wyckoff for "I Wish I Could Send You a Pocketful of Sunshine." Copyright © 2000 by Dolores Wyckoff. All rights reserved. Reprinted by permission.

A careful effort has been made to trace the ownership of poems used in this anthology in order to obtain permission to reprint copyrighted materials and give proper credit to the copyright owners. If any error or omission has occurred, it is completely inadvertent, and we would like to make corrections in future editions provided that written notification is made to the publisher:

BLUE MOUNTAIN ARTS, INC., P.O. Box 4549, Boulder, Colorado 80306.